I dedicate this book to my family, especially my grandma, Sylvia Lewgoy, who always encourages me and keep doodling and do my drawings.

Title: Luna and her friends - The pajama party
This is the first book in the "Luna and her friends" series.

Text copright©2024 by Sophia Laser
Illustrations copyright©2024 by Lewgoyillustrations
Revised by Peter Fox

All rights reserved. No part of this publication or product may be reproduced or stored in a retrieval system, or transmitted in any form or by any means, electronic, mechanical, recording, or otherwise, without written permission from the author.

Montreal, Canadá   ISBN: 978-1-0689142-0-1

Luna is a little girl full of imagination and ideas. She is always thinking of something cool to do with her friends. However, there is one interesting fact about Luna that you need to know. She loves pajamas!
When someone asks her: "what's your favorite gift?" She always answers:

pajamas!

She had a closet full of *pajamas* but she was never good at sharing.

2

One day, Luna had an idea and decided to ask her parents about it.

"Can I have a pajama party?"

Her parents thought a lot...

"Please!" said Luna.
"YES! But you need to tidy your room. It's a mess!" Mom and Dad agreed.

"For sure!" confirmed Luna.
"Okay! We are going to call their parents," they said.

Luna realized that there were many things to do starting with tidying her room.

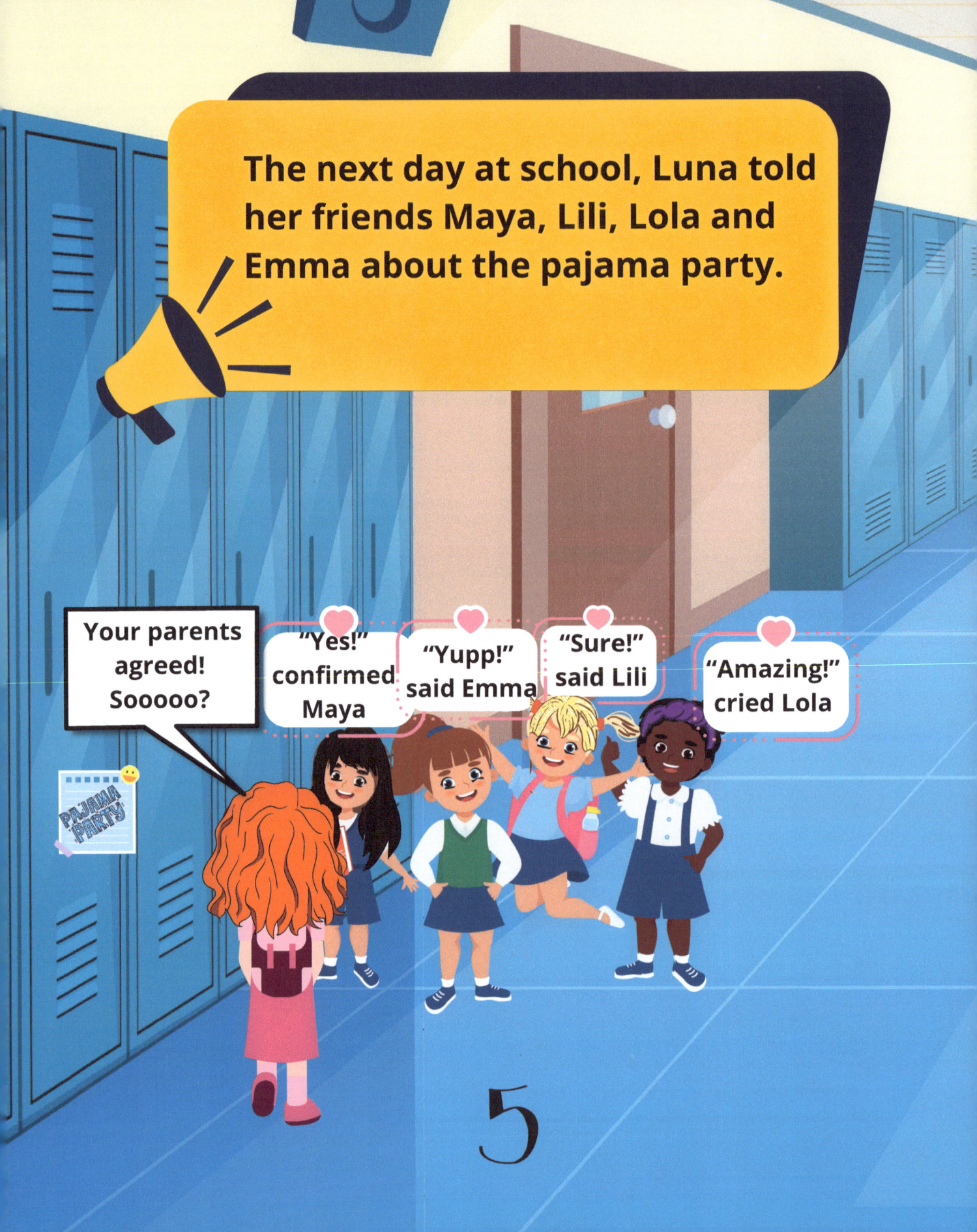

You are invited to my pajama party!
- Bring your favorite pajamas!
- There will be no overnight stay.

Address: 123 Blue Street

Date: Sunday 2023-09-03

from 15h to 18h

Luna prepared her bedroom to play with her friends. Her parents only helped with the snacks.

She took the girls to her favorite place at home... **her closet!**

Luna's mother couldn't believe what she was seeing.

Her daughter was learning to be kind and to share with her friends!

It's sure going to be a great pajama party!

Now, everybody calmed down.
The girls could choose ANY pajamas they wanted!

They were so happy! Everything she planned for the party was going well. The pillow fight, dancing, movies...

3 HOURS LATER...

15

Thank you for lending your pajamas!

We are happy that everything worked out.

Luna, you were incredible!

Adorable!

It was time to go home.

They were really tired.

Luna was exhausted!
Today was a fun day, but most importantly, she learned that sharing with friends is a lot more fun than she thought.

Luna's tips

Planning a Pajama Party

- Ask your parents if this is possible.
- Make a guest list.
- Write the invitations and deliver them.
- Prepare some snacks.
- Plan the activities: pillow fight, dancing, movies…
- Prepare the room.

Sophia Laser is 7 years old. She is Brazilian but has lived in Canada since she was 2. At this age, she began to make her first doodles.

As you can see, her favorite book character is Hermione Granger. Like Hermione, she likes to include her friends in her daily life. Her dream is to meet J. K. Rowling, the author of the Harry Potter book series.

At 4 years old, she was already drawing while watching the characters on TV. Now, Sophia plans to write her books and create characters.

This is the first in a series of books titled 'Luna and her friends'.

The family helps with her spelling and encourages her to read books and create stories.

www.ingramcontent.com/pod-product-compliance
Lightning Source LLC
Chambersburg PA
CBHW040101160426

43193CB00002B/37